The White Elephant

by Geraldine McCaughrean

illustrated by Gustavo Mazali

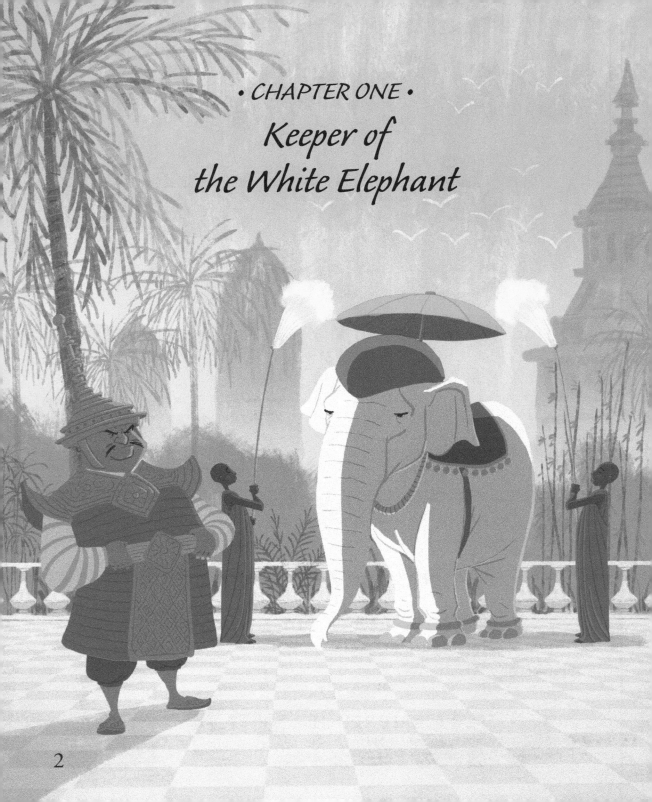

• CHAPTER ONE •
Keeper of the White Elephant

Once, in the kingdom of Siam, there was a king who was very rich indeed. He was born rich and he grew richer, chiefly because he never, ever gave anything away – no, not so much as a used tea-leaf. Unless you count his white elephant, of course.

White elephants are very rare. Few people have ever seen one. Far fewer have ever owned one. The king did not especially like his elephant, but he liked to own things that nobody else owned, and he liked to show off how rich he was. So he dressed the elephant in a saddle of scarlet velvet with golden tassels and a pink parasol to keep off the sun. There were gold bracelets for her ankles, a red leather hood and, around her neck, a silver chain.

He had a palace built for her, and ordered his servants to gather her food and fetch her water, to scrub her back and to fan her on hot days. Musicians and singers were sent to entertain her. Visitors to the palace marvelled at the wonderful beast, and the king was known on five continents as The King with the White Elephant. He liked to be famous. He was a vain man.

He was also spiteful. If one of his noblemen or advisors or generals annoyed him – did not bow low enough, forgot his birthday, lost a battle – he would smile and say, 'I shall make you my Keeper of the White Elephant. Take great care of her now, won't you?' It sounded like an honour. It was not.

That nobleman or advisor or general would have to take away the elephant, clothe her, feed her, build her a palace, entertain her and keep her clean. The cost would be terrible. The nobleman, advisor or general's money would soon be all gone. He would have to borrow from his friends, but would not be able to pay them back. His wife and children would go hungry. He would not sleep for worrying. He would grow shabby and ill. Finally, he would have to beg the king to take back his gift, then flee the country, shamed and penniless.

One day, the king tripped on the steps of his palace. Perhaps it was the fault of the steps. Perhaps the hot sun was to blame. Perhaps his big stomach unbalanced him, since he was very large. His courtiers squealed. His servants wailed and beat the steps with twigs.

Courtier Preecha helped the king to his feet. 'Your Majesty must rest,' he said, gently.

'Do you dare to say what the king must do?' blared the king.

'No, of course not. But your Majesty does not look well. I am sure a sleep would make you feel better,' and Preecha offered his arm for the king to lean on.

The king pushed him away. The other courtiers gasped and put their hands against their lips in horror. No one ever said the king looked less than wonderful. He was always 'a picture of health', 'as bright as the morning', 'the Glory of the World'.

'How kind,' said the king with a snarl. 'Do you hear? Courtier Preecha does not like the way the king looks. He wants the king to look better. We must reward him for his kindness. We shall make him Keeper of the White Elephant for two years, the lucky man. May the honour bring him joy.'

The other courtiers winced, as they knew it was no honour. Preecha knelt down and pressed his forehead to the floor. 'Your Highness is too kind to a humble nobody. My heart is filled with joy.'

'You poor thing,' said the Royal Flower Arranger.

'I am so sorry,' said the Royal Hairdresser.

'You did not deserve it,' said the Royal Writer of Letters. But secretly, they were glad. No white elephant for them!

Tucked up in bed, the king looked into his mirror and grinned his most wicked grin. He loved to punish courtiers who made him angry. He loved to make them beg and whimper and cry salt tears at the thought of the Royal White Elephant!

The fat face in the mirror turned from red to green. The king leaned out of bed and was sick on the floor. He had eaten too much for dinner. He really was feeling rather ill.

Preecha went to the Royal Elephant House to collect his gift. The Royal Grooms fetched the white elephant out of her palace into the sunlight. She blinked her pink eyes, dazzled. She was wearing a red velvet saddle cloth with golden tassels, gold bracelets on her ankles and a red leather hood. And rising from her saddle was a pink paper parasol to keep off the sun.

'She is more pink than white,' said Preecha thoughtfully. He took hold of the silver chain around her neck and led the elephant home to his house.

When Preecha's father saw him coming, the old man clutched at his grey hair and howled. 'Oh my poor boy! What brought this terrible fate upon your head?'

'I said the king looked unwell,' said Preecha cheerfully. 'Isn't she pink! I never realised white elephants were pink.'

Preecha's wife and children came running from the house.

'Elefump! Elefump!' said the little boy.

Preecha's father moaned. 'Now you will have to build a palace to keep the elephant in. Now you will have to pay one hundred servants to gather her food and fetch her water. Ten more to scrub her clean. Five more to fan her on hot days. Musicians and singers to entertain her. Now you will have to buy new saddle cloths of velvet, and gold tassels every week. The cost will ruin you. Your children will starve! Your life will be ruined! The King does this to his worst enemies. You did not deserve this.'

'She does really big poos, too,' said his daughter. 'The poos are not pink, though. She's nice.'

'She is, isn't she?' said Courtier Preecha. 'What shall we call her?

'Elefump!' said his little boy.

'Rosy,' said his daughter, 'because she is pretty and pink.'

'Where shall we build the palace?' Preecha's old father was dragging a heavy bag. 'This is all the money I have saved over the years. Have it. Of course, it is not enough.'

Preecha said, 'Tell me, because I am very stupid: in the wild, do elephants live in houses?'

His children giggled.

'Do they have a front door and a doormat? Do they take off their shoes and leave them by the door when they come home?'

His wife giggled, too.

'Do they have pictures on the wall and a stove with a fire in it?'

'But this is the king's Royal Elephant,' said his father, who again began to cry.

Preecha did not build a palace for the Royal White Elephant. He did not even build a barn. Instead, he led his elephant into his garden and said, 'You are our guest. There is a tree to keep off the sun. Here is a pond to drink from.' Then, he bowed to her.

Rosy blinked at him with her pink eyes. Her pale trunk smelled him from bottom to top. She blew his hair and watched it lift and fall back into place. Then she went and drank the pond dry. The fish flipped and flopped about in the mud. Preecha had to run to the house holding them in his two hands.

When he came back, Rosy was standing in the orchard.

'You are our guest. There is an apple tree. Here, a mulberry bush. There is an almond tree. Here is some bamboo.' Then, he bowed to her and left her alone. No one likes to be watched while they are eating.

When he came back, Rosy had eaten every nut, every piece of fruit, and most of the tree branches. She had eaten whole prickly bushes. The long grass had been pulled up and the bamboo was all gone. Her trunk brushed his sleeve and then his cheek.

Rosy led Preecha towards the gate, through it, and up to the summerhouse at the top of a grassy hill. In one direction lay the king's palace, in another, the jungle. Rosy lifted her trunk and trumpeted.

'You are our guest,' said Preecha. 'You must come and go as you please.'

Rosy blinked at him with her pink eyes. Her trunk coiled around his shoulders. She pulled his head close to hers. Her tusks were cool against his cheek. They stood together for a time. Then Rosy swayed away and away down the hill.

The new moon rose like the curved dagger the king wore at his wide, wide waist.

· CHAPTER THREE ·
Next Morning

Preecha's wife cried out in horror, 'You let her go? What about when the king hears that you have lost his white elephant? He will certainly cut off your head!'

Preecha said, 'Tell me, because I am very stupid: in the wild, do elephants dig gardens and grow their food?'

His daughter giggled.

'Do they stay indoors and read a book all day?'

His boy giggled, too. But his wife was much too frightened to laugh.

There was a noise of a fence falling down, a tree, too. They opened the door.

There stood the Royal White Elephant. Her red velvet saddle cloth was gone and so were her golden tassels. She did not have her silver chain, her golden bangles or her pink paper parasol. She was not white any more. She was not even pink. She was blobby brown and black and green from foraging in the jungle.

Preecha bowed to her. She blinked at him with her pink eyes. His son and daughter ran and hugged the elephant – one leg each. Their little arms hardly reached round. 'You came back!' they cried, joyfully.

Preecha's wife burst into tears. 'Now we must buy silver buckets and white cotton towels and pay ten men to wash her and dry her and spray her with precious perfume!'

Preecha pulled a strand of ivy off one tusk. 'Tell me, because I am very stupid: in the wild, do elephants fetch buckets and fill bathtubs and climb in and call a servant to wash behind their ears?'

The children laughed.

'Do elephants dry themselves with towels and spray themselves with perfume?'

Mrs Preecha did not laugh. 'You cannot send back a dirty elephant to the Royal Palace! We will all be boiled in oil!'

'So let us all go down to the river and swim,' said Preecha.

'Oh yes? Oh yes? And if she does not want to wash, what will you do? Carry her to the river and throw her in?'

But Preecha did not have to carry the elephant. He simply picked up an old broom and walked ahead of her. 'Come, Rosy. Come along.' Through the hole in the fence he went, and the elephant followed after.

When she heard the sound of water, Rosy began to trot. Preecha stepped aside and trotted after her. When he arrived, Rosy was already in the river, sucking water up her trunk. She squirted it over her back. When she shook her head, water drops flew from her ears like bits of torn-up sunshine. She was very happy.

'Elephants are clean animals,' Preecha told his children, swimming out from the shore. 'But everyone likes to have their back scrubbed.' And he climbed on to Rosy's back and brushed her with the broom. He sang as he brushed:

'Lovely Rosy, rosy pink,
How much water can you drink?
Can you drink the ocean dry?
Can you drink the sea-blue sky?'

Then Rosy sucked up a trunkful of water and sprayed Preecha, so that he slid over her tail and splashed into the river, giggling like a monkey.

Early every morning, before he went to the palace, Preecha rode his elephant to the river. Then she carried him home, and Preecha walked down to the palace and spent his day serving the king.

Rosy spent her day in the jungle, munching, mooching and thinking thoughts as big as elephants, inside her great head.

CHAPTER FOUR

Nearly Two Years Later

Once again, Preecha's old father fetched out his bag of money. He tipped it out on the floor. 'Son, son,' he said. 'Soon you must return the Royal White Elephant to the king. You must buy her a new saddle cloth of red velvet, bracelets for her ankles and new golden tassels. She must have a bridle of red leather, and a pink paper parasol … or we will all certainly be fed to the Royal Tigers!'

Preecha looked at the coins on the floor. 'Dear father, do you want me to use your money to buy such things? In the wild, do elephants wear bracelets? Do they wear robes? Do they wear hats or carry umbrellas?'

The children did not laugh. His wife did not laugh.

His father said, 'Soon, the king will send for his elephant, and he will expect golden bracelets, a leather hood, a red saddle cloth and a pink parasol. If Rosy is naked, the king will certainly turn us out of the kingdom.'

But Preecha did not hear him. He was sitting in front of his elephant, looking at her, his head on one side. 'Rosy,' he said. 'What have you been eating? You are almost as fat as the king!'

For 20 months, the king had watched Preecha as he did his work in the palace. The king waited for his courtier's hair to go grey with worry. He waited for Preecha to grow thin and ragged. Surely, by now, he had spent all his money on the Royal White Elephant? Richer men than Preecha had been ruined by the cost. But Preecha still looked happy. Richer men had come to the king and begged to return the white elephant to the Royal Stables. They had begged to be allowed to leave Siam before their children starved.

The king could not sleep any more, but lay awake thinking about Preecha's happy, smiling face, his cheerful singing. When the king ate his supper, he was thinking always: why is Preecha not starving?

28

Perhaps Preecha had secret hoards of gold!

Perhaps he had been stealing from the Royal Treasury!

Perhaps he was being helped by the other courtiers – or by enemies of the king!

Perhaps Preecha had killed the white elephant to save himself from ruin!

The king sat up in bed and, though it was midnight, began to shout: 'Guards! Guards! Send for Courtier Preecha! Tell him I want my elephant back by noon tomorrow. If he is one minute late, he dies!'

Preecha did not laugh when he got the message. He told his children, and they were sad, too.

His wife and father were terrified. 'No time to buy new! No time for the goldsmiths and the parasol-maker, and the tailor and the saddler to make new! Oh, oh! What will become of us?'

But Preecha only walked up to their summerhouse on the hill. He fetched out the red velvet saddle cloth, the golden bracelets and the golden tassels. He fetched out the red leather bridle and the pink parasol. 'I took them off Rosy the day I let her go free.'

Now, though, he must put them back on her. Rosy would not like it. One last bath in the river, he thought, and went into the early morning garden.

But Rosy did not greet him with a wave of her trunk. She was kneeling under the cherry tree, moaning.

'Bath time, Rosy!'

'Hmmggmmnungh,' said the elephant, and rolled onto her side.

'Come quick, wife!' called Preecha. 'Our elephant is ill!'

Rosy lurched onto her knees again and clambered
to her feet. She swayed and rocked and roared and pushed
him with her great forehead so that he crashed over
backwards. 'She knows I have come to take her back to
the palace, and her great heart is broken!'

Rosy heaved herself up, huge in the little garden.
He offered her bamboo, but she threw it on the grass.
She gave one great bellow.

'Come, family! I think our elephant is dying!'

They all came running.

Meanwhile, the king sat on his throne, scowling. Why was Preecha still happy when he should be miserable? Why was the Royal Stable still empty of elephant? Why had the courtier not come begging for mercy? Why had he not brought back the Royal White Elephant?

The whole sun rose above the horizon. The morning grew warm. Insects buzzed.

The morning grew hot. Apples fell from the apple trees.

The sun rose almost to the top of the sky, and still Preecha did not come.

In the Royal Palace, the king stamped his feet. He thumped his fists on the arms of his throne. 'I WANT MY ELEPHANT!' he shouted. 'NOW!'

The cups and plates rattled in the Royal Kitchen.

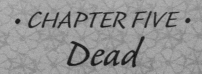

· CHAPTER FIVE ·
Dead

It was just after noon when Preecha arrived. He was all alone. No elephant walked beside him. No trunk held his hand. He did not want to die; he wanted to run away. But that would not be honourable. No, he had to tell the king.

The palace was silent. The only sounds were the slap of his feet and the thump-thump-thump of his heart.

'The king wishes to see me,' he told the priest standing by the door of the throne room.

'The king will not see you now,' said the priest. 'You have come too late.'

'I know. I was delayed. I hope the king will forgive me.'

'He will not,' said the priest.

Preecha bowed his head sadly. 'No, I suppose not.'

'This morning, the king shouted too loudly. He stamped too hard. He raged too hotly. His face grew too red. He died of a bad temper.'

'Oh!' said Preecha.

'The fate of a man cannot be changed,' said the priest. 'Where is the Royal White Elephant?'

For a moment, Preecha could not speak.
Then, he covered his face with his sleeve.
He seemed to be crying. 'That is why
I am late. Elephants are wise. Elephants are
mysterious. Elephants know things we do
not know. The Great White Elephant surely
knew the king was dead, because she died of
grief this morning.'

'Oh,' said the priest.

'The fate of an elephant cannot be changed,'
said Preecha.

He ran all the way back to his house.
He ran past the river, calling as he ran.
'Wife! Children! Honoured father! I told
a little lie today. I knew Rosy was not dead!
Forgive me. But look, I, too, am not dead!'
He ran through the hole in the fence
and into his trampled garden.

There stood Rosy the White Elephant
and beside her a grey baby elephant,
blinking its brown eyes.

'Oh, you did it! Well done, Rosy! That is
 an excellent baby elephant!'

After many happy days with Rosy and her baby, came a sad day for Preecha. His father, his wife, his children all wept. Preecha wiped his eyes. 'Tell me,' he said, 'because I am very stupid: in the wild, do elephants live in palaces or gardens or in one place?'

'No, Daddy.'

'In the wild, do elephants live with people and send their babies to school?'

'No, husband.'

'In the wild, are elephants the kings and queens of the animal kingdom? Do they wear the wind between their ears, the rain on their backs, and the sky for a parasol?'

'Yes, son,' said his father. Rosy nodded, too. She rested her trunk on her baby's head.

'And that is why we must say goodbye.'

They led their friends down to the river. They all swam across to the edge of the jungle. Then Preecha and his family watched mother and calf plunge into the darkness of the trees.

Into the wild.

The White Elephant ❦ Geraldine McCaughrean

Teaching notes written by Sue Bodman and Glen Franklin

Using this book

Content/theme/subject

In this story, Preecha is handed a White Elephant as a punishment, but his good sense and honesty lead to a positive outcome. This book is written in the style of a traditional story, incorporating many of those features. Events occur over time, illustrating the changing fortunes and intentions of the main characters. The story itself plays on the notion of a 'White Elephant' as a possession or gift that is difficult or expensive to maintain.

Language structure

- Literary phrases are used to enhance the traditional style, such in as the repetition of 'Tell me, for I am very stupid'.
- Implied events to come, for example: 'The new moon rose like the curved dagger the king wore at his wide, wide waist.' (p.16).

Book structure/visual features

- Chapter headings delineate both the passing of time ('Next Morning'; 'Nearly Two Years Later') and significant shifts in events ('Dead') to engage the reader.

Vocabulary and comprehension

- Vocabulary choices portray the use of irony. For example, on p.6, the king is not really rewarding Preecha, but punishing him for speaking his mind.
- Effective verb choice supports characterisation, for example in helping the reader identify with the king's true intention (p33).

Curriculum links

Natural history – Elephants are an endangered species under threat from hunting and poaching for their ivory tusks. Children could investigate true life examples of conservation projects set up to preserve and protect elephants living in the wild.

Learning outcomes

Children can:

- use the key points of a story to summarise events over time
- identify authorial techniques which use grammatical structures to position the reader
- evaluate word choice, for example in the use of figurative or emotive language.

Planning for guided reading

Lesson One Characterisation through vocabulary choice

Introduce the new book by asking the children to predict the type of text this will be, giving rationales for their decisions. Discuss other traditional tales they have read and consider the characteristics (setting in the past; good triumphs over evil; etc.).

Share with the children the meaning of a 'White Elephant'. Look at and compare dictionary definitions, and ask the children to explain their understanding of the phrase with you. Use the definitions, the front cover of the book and the blurb on the back to predict what might happen in the story.

Ask the children to read pages 2 and 3 to themselves. Then discuss what is known of the king, by referring to specific vocabulary ('He was a vain man'; 'He was also spiteful').

Use p.4 to explore what happened when the king got annoyed with his advisors and generals. Does this fit with the children's understanding of a White Elephant from their discussions?

Set an independent reading task to read to p.10. Listen in whilst children read, drawing attention to vocabulary choices that depict characterisation and aid comprehension. For example, on p9, Preecha speaks 'cheerfully' even though the king has given him the White Elephant as a punishment. What does this tell the reader about Preecha?